LOW
CENTRE OF
GRAVITY

ALSO BY MICHAEL DENNIS:

quarter on it's edge (Fast Eddie Press, 1979)
sometimes passion, sometimes pain (Ordinary Press, 1982)
no saviour and no special grace (South Western Ontario Poetry, 1983)
poems for jessica-flynn (Not One Cent of Subsidy Press, 1986)
so you think you might be judas (Privately published, 1987)
Wayne Gretzky in the house of the sleeping beauties (Lowlife Publishing, 19⋅
Portrait (Dollarpoems/Brandon University, 1988)
Fade to Blue (Pulp Press, 1988)
what we remember and what we forget (Bobo Press, 1993)
missing the kisses of eloquence (General Store Publishing House, 1994)
the on-going dilemma of small change (above/ground press, 1995)
what we pass over in silence (above/ground, 1996)
no gravy, no garlands, no bright lights (Privately published, 1999)
This Day Full of Promise: Poems Selected and New (Broken Jaw Press, 200⋅
All Those Miles Yet to Go (LyricalMyrical Press, 2005)
Poems for Another Poetry Reading (LyricalMyrical, 2006)
Arrows of Desire (General Store Publishing House, 2006)
forgiveness, my new sideline (Proper Tales Press, 2009)
Coming Ashore on Fire (Burnt Wine Press, 2009)
Smile (Burnt Wine Press, 2009)
Watching the Late Night Russian News in the Nude (Burnt Wine Press, 200⋅
On Being a Dodo (Burnt Wine Press, 2009)
How Are You She Innocently Asked (Apt. 9 Press, 2010)
The Uncertainty of Everything (Burnt Wine Press, 2011)
A Tiresome Litany of Indignities (Proper Tales Press, 2014)
Talking Giraffes (Phafours, 2015)
Bad Engine: New & Selected Poems (Anvil Press, 2017)
The Dagmar Poems (w/ Stuart Ross; Burnt Wine Press, 2017)
Sad Balloon (Monk Press, 2019)
Divining (Proper Tales Press, 2019)
Caterwaul: Nine Poems (shreeking violet press, 2019)
The President of the United States (above/ground press, 2019)
MDSR (w/ Stuart Ross; Sunday Afternoon Poems, 2019)
Spøkjelse i japanske drosjar/Ghosts in Japanese Taxis (A + D, 2020)

LOW
CENTRE OF
GRAVITY

MICHAEL DENNIS

ANVIL PRESS • VANCOUVER • 2020

Anvil Press Publishers Inc.
P.O. Box 3008, Main Post Office
Vancouver, B.C. V6B 3X5 CANADA
www.anvilpress.com

Library and Archives Canada Cataloguing in Publication

Title: Low centre of gravity / Michael Dennis.
Names: Dennis, Michael, 1956- author.
Description: First edition. | Poems.
Identifiers: Canadiana 20200241087 | ISBN 9781772141542 (softcover)
Classification: LCC PS85573.E563 L69 2020 | DDC C811/.54—dc23

Edited by Stuart Ross
Cover design by Rayola.com
Cover art by Eliza Griffiths
Interior by HeimatHouse
Author photo by Stuart Ross

Represented in Canada by Publishers Group Canada
Distributed by Raincoast Books

The publisher gratefully acknowledges the financial assistance of the Canada Council for the Arts, the Canada Book Fund, and the Province of British Columbia through the B.C. Arts Council and the Book Publishing Tax Credit.

We acknowledge the financial support of the Government of Canada through the National Translation Program for Book Publishing for our translation activities.

PRINTED AND BOUND IN CANADA

For Kirsty

"When God punishes you, it's not that you don't
get what you want. It's that you get everything
that you want, but there's no time left."
—Miles Davis

TABLE OF CONTENTS

WINTER STORM

the falling snow is beautiful but
we're only inches from doom

the car ahead can't stop
and neither can the one behind us

we need a miracle
and that shop is closed for the night

Susan and Tony saw time expand
as though a car had always

been following them
in the blink of four eyes

their lives sped past
they remembered many of the same things

but not in the same order
impact was musical then catastrophic

both of their memories
stopped at the same time

Susan remembered an old boyfriend and smiled
Tony wondered where his bicycle was

hey didn't go to heaven
ven though they were both kind

they went to the Holy Rosary Hill Cemetery
laid out side by side

although at home
Susan was always on the left

THE CYCLIST

you see the young woman
pedalling quickly
up and down the street
this happens
several times a day

you think
there must be a methadone clinic
within a few minutes' walk
but it is an uninformed guess

nonetheless
she always looks sad
heading in at least
one direction

WITNESSES

we are the selfish ruin
on the fresh cut grass

a dark wind caresses our dreams
as fiery eyes watch

I feel hampered by witnesses
but I am nothing

and you are nothing
it's not unusual

something will happen soon enough

TOMBSTONE

walked into a reading last week
shot the unsuspecting poet
right between his surprised eyes

picked the mic out of the air
the dead guy wouldn't need it
and rattled off my latest poem

the audience was lukewarm at best
but I still had some bullets
and they would all love me soon

GHOSTS IN JAPANESE TAXIS ·

my lovely wife loves whisky
but it only makes me want to cry

I start thinking about ghosts
and how they haunt Japanese taxis
tsunami victims trying to get home

I start dreaming I'm Syrian
I own a small barbershop
my children are in school
my wife works at a grocer's
at night, even in my dreams
we laugh long and hard

whisky makes me weep
I drink red, Italian
the blood of the Gods
of legionnaires, gladiators, slaves
that empire as corrupt as any
that makes monuments to itself

I'm happy
while the rest of the world
unfurls in flame

LAST AT BAT

I remembered the right thing
then didn't do it
because I was hungry or lazy
my selfish self sucked in the day
as though I owned it
as though the sun rose for me alone

next door the dog lounged on the porch
licked his own balls
just because he could

two doors away
the mailman approached

DAMNED POETS

the new bookcase
simple unfinished pine planks
makes me happier
than any piece of wood should

I spend my days
in this study
thousands of poets
staring out at me from the shelves
all of them shouting

you'd think they could agree on something
but they don't agree on a damned thing

CHEMO DUCK AND COUPLE

it was the parking lot of a big hospital
and I was waiting for my chemo friend
the duck was doing what ducks do
sitting just off the sidewalk

an older couple walked by
her pushing him in a wheelchair
an oxygen tank riding piggyback
I knew he wanted my smoke
as soon as I looked him in the eye
I smiled to say I was sorry

when they noticed the duck
the couple stopped their slow roll
and took up residence on the grass
a few feet from the creature
it was a beautiful morning
for some of us

the minutes passed and we four
sat there in silence waiting
for the next thing

THE BEST PEOPLE

*"The best people possess a feeling for beauty, the
courage to take risks, the discipline to tell truth,
the capacity for sacrifice. Ironically, their virtues
make them vulnerable, they are often wounded,
sometimes destroyed."*

—Ernest Hemingway

Andy comes to our door
every three or four weeks
he trails a hockey bag
which he fills
with the bottles and cans
we've saved just for him

Andy is a bit younger than me
let's say he's 40
his wife died last winter
he didn't say of what

Andy is always as polite as church
used to be a short-order cook
but I don't think he cooks much now
his sorrow is no worse than many
it is his private burden
he's what I call a toiling optimist
his happy diligence inspires me

I imagine teenage Andy
dancing with his teenage wife
all their future yet to be danced
all those stars, all that hope
up in that dark, dark sky

CHINESE FOOD WITH STUART ROSS

so I'm sitting beside the poet Stuart Ross
and we are looking out at Lovesick Lake

neither of us could have
imagined this scene
even a short time ago

we have been on a boat for three days
with our splendid wives
we are all sailors now

we started on Pigeon Lake
rounded Big Island
then ventured to Buckhorn

in Buckhorn
we went to the same Chinese restaurant
Kirsty and I went to the last time
we were in Buckhorn
Stuart absolutely befuddled
when I asked our waitress for chopsticks
and she responded "I'll have to see"
as though it was the first time
she'd ever been asked that question

Stuart and Laurie liked their egg foo young
and we all agreed
the egg rolls were excellent

it wasn't the first time
Stuart and I had Chinese food together
but one of the best

MISS TWISTLETON'S STARS

under the covers last night
my wife reading a novel
and I'm reading a book of poems
the poems are first-rate
which always lightens my mood
when K turns a page
the duvet and sheet
drift below her perfect breast
and I reach over
softly draw a quick star
on the side of her breast
K is only partly amused

later when she has entered
the world of the sleeping
and turned over on her stomach
I delicately ink a second star
on her second perfect breast
the stars are smaller than a dime
in the style I learned
from my grade 3 teacher
Miss Twistleton

SMOKING IN THE LANEWAY

although I picked worms as a child I don't give them
much thought these days but this spring I've noticed
legions of them on our asphalt laneway I've started
picking them up and dropping them in our front garden
I watch the worms as I smoke and it is the same thing
every time—for 30 seconds or so there is no movement
at all then one end of the worm twitches closer to the
earth, moves in a dark rhythm that knows where soil will
give way and a small portion of the worm is swallowed
by terra firma

the worms slow coil in stop motion as they swim into
the earth one spasm at a time the ash on my smoke also
slow curling into smoke before it disappears

WENT TO ANOTHER FUNERAL

went to another funeral last week
a young woman, 53
had a sore stomach one day
six weeks later, gone

this woman worked with my wife
several years ago
and they had become friends
the death unsettled K
who is now 55

we've learned almost everything
over the millennia
we've travelled to the stars
and the bottom of the ocean
but we've learned so little
about death

this 53-year-old woman
had an open coffin
and so did my 83-year-old aunt Dora
died just a few weeks ago

my uncle Dan was 73
he's been gone two months
he was cremated right away

no idea what happened
to my aunt Alice
she was in her late 70s
and died four months back
there was no service for her
of any kind

sometimes the responsibilities
that accompany death
are simply too much to bear
we lumber through
what we don't have the skills to handle
the weight of it
worse than gravity
some call it
time

MR. DAYNES

don't know what bee
Mr. Daynes had in his bonnet
but he didn't cut his son much slack

I never liked Scott much either
he was always pushing me around
though I forget why

this one time Scott and I were arguing
so Mr. Daynes made us
put on some old boxing gloves
and settle the score like gentlemen

Scott had three or four inches on me
but I had 20 or 30 pounds
of muscle on him

I walked through his flailing
and dropped what I had on him
Mr. Daynes didn't let me beat on his son
for too long
but I'd certainly tenderized him

Scott never bothered me again
after that day
but I've often wondered
what he thought of his dad
that day and since

that day when his dad
patted me on the back
said "Good job, son"
while I stood
over the prone young boy
rage and fear
both shaking in my bones

WAITING IN THE AIRPORT

I am waiting for K
her flight is late
the airport busier than usual

this weekend
she was in Toronto
with her sisters

while I spent a quiet time
home alone

went to bed early each night
a small stack of books in hand

our air-conditioner screaming
in the window

when K is away
I always kiss my wedding ring

before I turn out the light
a silly ritual

but it reminds me
of what is important

makes me say her name
before dreaming

our quiet life together
the opposite of a busy airport

someone is always
headed home

and someone
is always waiting

TOM THOMSON SHIT IN THE WOODS

then he opened up his satchel
his box of paints and panels
and painted

you can't see the dirty hands
of the men who cut the trails
laid the tracks
or the women who fed them
but they are all in there

it's hard to see
an ocean crossing
or Grosse Isle
but they are present

behind every beautiful tree
carved into every
scenic rock

the effort to imagine beauty as simple as
one foot in front of the other
into every ecstatic sunset

Thomson may not
have intended any of it
ass deep in muskeg

how many mosquitoes and blackflies
do you imagine are buried
in the muscular stabs of paint
he carted out
one stomp through the woods
at a time

THE BEAR

not after Marian Engel

it was mid-morning on our third day at the cottage when
my wife pointed it out to me

near the stairs to the deck closest to the BBQ two neat
fresh piles of bear scat

last night I had revealed with some shame that I was
afraid of the dark at the cottage

from our long history together my wife knows I have an
unreasonable fear of bears and sharks

bears are sharks of the forest   sharks, bears of the sea

anyway, my wife joined me in the Georgian Bay darkness
so I could smoke my last of the night

we chatted a few minutes and then I could not see her
until she lurched out of the pitch yelling "BOO!"

I bear-danced backwards much to her pleasure my fear
palpable in the air and then she yelled "BEAR!!"

I bolted past her tried to run through the closed screen
to her screams of mirth

an hour or so after my darling K delighted in showing me the scat she decided to have a shower and I decided to get even

I made myself as bear-big as I could outside the bathroom door   I imagined I was a bear and could hear her shuffling just feet away

my bear nose could smell her sweet smells as I rose to the ops of my bear toes

vhen I heard the door start to open I gave her my best bear oar and she slashed out at the air between us equal parts urprised and pissed

shot outside as fast as my little bear legs would take me

hatever bear awaited me out there I knew my chances ere better than where I'd just been

PORCUPINE

first thing I think of when I think of porcupines
is my stint at the Museum of Civilization

I'd always been proud of my left-wing liberalism
comfortable with my grasp of racism

and then I started working with the
Aboriginal collections

at first I didn't make the connections
as I sorted the elaborate spoons
and astonishing rattles
I recognized the historical significance
only in terms of settler history
no connection to the now

somehow I'd accepted
without question
my grandfather's white man's conception
of a "cowboy and injun" red man

working with everyday objects or sacred relics
it was always the same
I was astonished and enthralled by the technical skill
the utilitarian simplicity
the mastery of craft and design
and the human beauty these people incorporated
into every part of their lives

the longer I worked in the First Nations Collection
the more I was reminded of how little we learned
while busy stealing everything they had

those moccasins in the shoe store in the mall
they have plastic straws cut to resemble porcupine quill
Big Chief Slippers—Size 8½
stamped on the bottom

somewhere in the woods near a stream and a lake
a porcupine and a beaver crossed paths
both thinking how odd the other looked

THE GROUP OF SEVEN

no one ever called them that
to their faces
no one would dare

since grade six
Steve the "Hammer," "Eddie," "Spit"
the MacDonald Twins—
"Heckle" and "Jeckle"—
Bobby, who we named "Skipper"
because he had a stammer
skipped every other word
and Joe Joe Donelly
hung out together
morning, noon and night

if you were stupid enough
to annoy any one of them
you'd annoyed them all

everyone in our neighbourhood knew
not to draw the Group's attention
and secretly prayed and publicly wailed
for them to leave home
or be locked up

it was a girl named Sally
that killed the Group of Seven
Joe Joe liked her first
Skipper liked her most

but it was Eddie that got the girl
Eddie was a good talker for a quiet guy
but not a great fighter
Joe Joe swung at him one Friday night
just before Thanksgiving
the year they were in grade eleven

Heckle and Jeckle
tried to get between
Joe Joe and Eddie
Spit held off the Skipper
and that was it

a week later
Eddie's got a new haircut
walks down the street
holding Sally's hand

the Hammer drives by
with Bobby riding shotgun
they are heading the other direction
nobody says a word

from that day on
n our neighbourhood
he Group of Seven
vere just a bunch of old painters

FRASS

I knew, like most of us
that bees make honey
but it wasn't until this morning
that I saw a bee poop

it all had to do with the lighting
where the bee was
in relation to me
and the sun

I often watch the bees
as they industry their way
through our garden

this particular striped hovercraft
took off from the top
of a stalk of dead day lily
and out over the laneway

and that's when I saw it
beads of bee scat
popping out the bee's ass
a retreating helicopter
spraying bullets in its wake

I had to think about it for a minute
to be sure of what I had witnessed
I am over 60
and had never seen this before

I looked it up on the internet
who knew

of course it only stands to reason
a biological machine
where food enters one end
and is eventually ejected
through some sort of hole
on the other

turns out that bee poop
is made mostly of pollen husks
and good beekeepers
monitor the health of their hives
by checking the bees' droppings

strange comfort
in learning this little more
about the world around me
how bees have screen-like filters
in their abdomens
to help in the nectar/pollen/poop process
stuff like that

when this morning's
improbable flying object
um-spit onto my laneway
wasn't thinking of the
disintegrating American empire

or any of the horrors
currently burning
in other parts of the world

I forgot we stole this country
from those who were here
before us

I forgot the poverty of others
the corruption
of the rich

when the pooping bee
heliported off our garden
and spat missile goo
on our laneway
it made me
chuckle to my desk
just to tell you

THERE IS NO RESPONSIBILITY ONCE YOU ARE DREAMING

had an inappropriate dream last night
about the wife of an old friend
she'd never visited me sleeping before
but she certainly made herself at home

not much really happened
mostly innuendo and promise
but I woke up feeling guilty

it happens like that
people I haven't seen in ages
marching right across my frontal cortex
as though they'd been there all along

I smell the Chanel vapour
mixed in with the heat of her skin
and all seems possible

I wake up before fireworks
and am all guilty for nothing at all
smell my hands for proof
grin like I just got out of jail

I think of calling my old friend
on the off chance he won't be home

OTONABEE INN

we've stayed at this particular hotel
at least a dozen times
it's close to my sister's place
and we know the sheets will be clean

when you get a room at the back
you can watch the ducks in the estuary
and the squirrels chasing blue jays away

the second-last time we stayed there
my sister from my father's second marriage
was staying there as well
with her adult children
all of us in town
for the funeral of an aunt we loved

at a house party that evening
I somehow insulted the illiterate nephew
of my sister-once-removed
how was I to know that at 22
he could not read

I'd written something down
for him and he
lost his mind
his anger was immediate
he promised violence

it did not end
until after the threats of fists
and guns
and the interjection of others

the party was ruined
and we left shortly after

the next morning in the motel parking lot
I ran into my sister again
she apologized for her son's behaviour
and I accepted to make her feel better

I knew I'd enjoy our old motel better
the next time we were there

and that's what happened:
the ducks in the water
and squirrels on the lawn
no angry relatives
in any room
of the Otonabee Inn

DRIVING CAROL

once every six weeks
I drive the 45 minutes
out to Barhaven
to pick up Carol
my mother-in-law Ann's oldest friend
and bring her back to Ottawa
to have lunch with Ann

Carol still looks sharp at 86
you can see clearly
that her beauty had been unworldly

along the way
Carol tells me about the men
who live in her seniors residence
how they fall for her
like wounded teenagers
Carol is tired of men though
and laughs as she tells me
how they crumble at her feet

three hours after I drop Carol
off at Ann's for lunch
I pick her up and drive her back
to her residence in Barhaven
another 45 minutes

Carol, a little drunk before dinner
tells me again
about the octogenarians who swoon
in the retirement residence's halls

as she walks, walkerless
to her quiet room
where she doesn't have to listen
to men anymore

THE BLUE BLUE SKY

I only ever climbed one mountain in my life
and I never wanted to do anything like it again

it was no Everest, being a Canadian mountain
but it still took us almost two days
to reach the top

about halfway up
I dropped a water bottle
and watched it fall
for a full 15 seconds

I suggested quitting at one point
having reached the end of my curiosity
but my partner would have no part of it
demanded I summon a stronger part of myself
he had to settle for the other

I couldn't quit and could barely go on
but we eventually reached the summit
we hadn't said much for hours

I asked him to forgive my earlier moment of fear
he was smiling when he took my hand
"nothing to forgive now" he said
gesturing to the blue blue sky
above us
and below

SLAM DUNK

you are halfway through
what you are convinced is a great poem
when you realize you've just repeated the plot
of a recent famous movie
there is nothing new in your treatment of the story

you have been poring over this poem all morning
taking it in a little here
letting out the seam a little there

and you are closing in on the killer ending
when the movie star who plays the lead
appears all movie-star technicolour
right in the middle of the poem
looks you in the eye
until you feel counterfeit

fist crumble the offending evidence
lean back and Michael Jordan that damned thing
into the garbage can beside your desk

MARCOLIANI MILANO SOCKS

you wake up one morning and you're in the Mafia

but your parents are from Ireland
and yesterday you were teaching grade five
at Prince of Wales Public School
and had to stay late because
Johnny River wrote in oil pastel
on the chalkboard

the morning you wake up in the Mafia
you wake up with a brunette in your bed
although you've never seen her before
she seems certain she knows you

you see your gun in its holster
hanging over the bedpost
your fancy linen suit on the chair

yesterday you were wearing work socks
and heavy leather sandals
that you had picked up on holiday in Mexico

today it is Marcoliani Milano
silk stockings
Fratelli Rossetti shoes

you look out the window
and see
the big black sedan, no sign of your Mini

you finish dressing
put on the holster
wait to see
what happens next

FORTUNE COOKIE

it's your father's birthday
and he is 90 years old
he spends the day with his family
there is an outing
with sunshine and laughter

that afternoon
you have cake with
multitudinous candles
90 to be exact
gathered family
help you blow them out

dinner is your favourite
Chinese food delivered from Yang Sheng
neon sweet-and-sour pork
chicken-fried rice with peas

you are sitting at the head of the table
you pass food and laugh at jokes
smile at your children, their children
their children

at the end of the meal
when people are ready to leave the table
one of your daughters cannot wake you
to open your fortune cookie
your final fortune
just told

FOURTH ARRONDISSEMENT

we walked in
and were directed to two seats
where two seats didn't appear to be
front and centre
but the French jazz crowd parted
with welcoming smiles
and our drinks arrived too

the singer was inches away
and pretending she loved me

as much as my wife allowed me
I loved her back

the music warmed the cavernous little club
and our feet tapped Paris time
Edith Piaf was in a back corner
sipping Pernod and hacking a Gauloises
Bud Powell was rubbing her back

later, when we were on our way
back to our walkup in Fourth Arrondissement
we imagined our footsteps echoing like
Hemingway's or Miller's

when in truth we sounded
exactly like every other drunk tourist
happy in the Parisian night

MY BIG MOUTH

I didn't necessarily want trouble
but I suppose yelling
"you stink
like shit's poorer, sadder cousin"
wasn't going to cheer him up

I'd been around the block
with this guy before

and was just as happy
to see him walk away

my big mouth
never doing me
any favours

MY WEDDING RINGS

our first wedding rings were "puzzle rings" made of silver we bought them from a street vendor at a marketplace in Istanbul they only cost a few lira but they meant everything to us

we married a year later still loving our Turkish travel rings

a few years after that my ring broke and we decided to replace silver with gold our gold puzzle rings really suited us

then a few years ago K took her ring to the jeweller to be resized but that night the jewellery shop burned to the ground along with the rest of the block

tried replacing K's ring—had the jeweller in on the search—but our lack of success took us through the calendar

in the end I brought my gold puzzle ring to the same, relocated jeweller I asked him to take the four separated rings from the original and make them into two rings one for each of us

the puzzle part of the ring no longer works each of us has two rings melted together the separate rings welded so they can never come apart

we've had our new gold rings a few years now it's astonishing how quickly the years fly past   time the only gold that matters

QUIET FUTURE

I used to read the newspapers
but there's nothing in them anymore
I used to watch the late-night news
but I no longer stay up late

I listen to old music
and remember
how we walked those late-night back streets
as though our shadows were giants

we marched
from street light
to street light
silently sailing
toward
our quiet future

MY OTHER LIFE

she was wearing nothing but a whalebone corset and a smile
when she opened the door
it was winter and the frigid air
popped her nipples to attention
it was one of the better welcomes I'd yet encountered

she had started a fire in the stove
and dragged her mattress to the living room floor
had the room draped in candles
a bottle of red beside the mattress

it was liberating to know my purpose
as I stumbled out of my winter clothes
by the time I reached the mattress
she'd sparked up a burner to share

the rest of this story played out
almost exactly as you'd imagine
we burned out those candles
our particulars only slightly different than yours

I think of nights like this one
once in a while
my other life
that other time

GETTING IT UP

just wrote a poem about sex when I was a younger man
and although the sex was good the poem was crap
my old friend Michael Newman told me
more than 30 years ago
to quit writing about my small life
I'm starting to think he was right

I'm getting ready to tackle
the bigger issues of the day
like the evil rat bastard Trump
and his pissy Russian connections

how all of North America
was murdered from those
who were here first
generations of Aboriginal people
evicted and eviscerated

how nations were built
on the backs of slave labour

how the miserable and evil rich
will the poor to death for profit

the racist religious right
foaming at the mouth
with the same vigour
as any other cult

I'm going to take it all on
because that's what poets do
when we can't get it up
anymore

WHAT I WAS LOOKING FOR

I was a young man on the road
with no idea where I was going
and only a slight idea of where I'd been

that summer I hitchhiked all over southern Ontario
London, Peterborough, Nilestown, Sharbot Lake
just to name a few stops
looking for a place to land

people were polite
but it's not like anyone
had any answers

I was welcomed
but got no invitations
to stay

it's not that others don't care
but they are invested elsewhere
they wish you no harm
but your problems are not theirs

that feeling of being lost
in a familiar world
never really went away
until I met her

she's upstairs on the couch
in our living room
while I watch the playoffs
in the basement

this little part of the world
what I was looking for
all the time

HISTORY

once spent an afternoon at a jazz concert held in the same field as the Battle of Bull Run

had a Saturday afternoon driving through Croatia where we came upon field after field surrounded with bright red skull-and-crossbone signs—vivid warning that the fields were filled with mines

I crossed the Maginot Line while driving outside of Strasbourg, where we were staying in a convent on the top of a mountain—the convent was ringed with a stone wall and in the stone wall were buried clerics and priests, saints and sinners

and one time while in Wales I walked through the craggy remains of Castell Dinas Brân where some historians tell us a young prince whose crime was another man was butt-fucked with a red-hot spit until he cooked to death from the inside

his corpse didn't have a mark on it

FUNERAL CHAT

my aunt Dora died last week
but I hadn't seen her in three years
the last time
was at my aunt Ethel's funeral

Aunt Dora's funeral was in Oshawa
and when I walked into the wake
I heard my aunt Sharon say
"There's Michael"

I'd seen Aunt Sharon recently
my uncle Dan, her husband
died a couple of weeks ago
I showed up at his funeral
the way I always show up

my aunt Kathryn was also at Aunt Dora's wake
so was my aunt Ella

I hadn't seen any of my cousins
in over four decades
but three of them
were at the wake

there's no way around 40 years of small talk
and after we'd said our hellos
there was dead air
in the same room as my dead aunt

I remembered the small East City home
where we'd all played as children
how Sam and Pam Crowe
lived happily next door

then we all smiled
and not another word was said

all those years
had said them for us

MY FAVOURITE SCENE IN THE GODFATHER

in the movie *The Godfather*
we find out very little
about Sonny Corleone's lover
once Sonny dies

we don't see her again
until she shows up
as Andy Garcia's mother
in *The Godfather Part III*

Mario Puzo gave her more time in his novel
we learn about her medical condition, her difficulties
her life after Sonny's sad trip to the toll booth
we meet the doctor who repairs her
from the inside out

Sonny Corleone climbing the stairs of the family home
at the wedding of his younger sister Connie
then the pounding against the bedroom door
much to the amusement of a staid Tom Hagen

Sonny Corleone descending the stairs
of a lipstick-stained lover
while his henchmen read dime novels
it on uneasy steps
pistols digging into their sides

my favourite moments in a film
where almost everybody
ends up dead

SIXTY-ONE

it might be Johnny Rivers singing
The Poor Side of Town
or the rain that's been falling
for six days

but the roof seems lower
the walls are closing in

it feels like I've been 60
a lot longer
than 60 years

last week
it snowed

and now the sun is too hot
for me to sit on the front porch

AFTER CLOSING TIME

and before she went home
to her husband
Angela used to come by

I didn't have to do a thing
I'd just leave the door unlocked
and a light on in the hall

I'd usually be asleep
only waking
when she crawled in
between the sheets

later, when she'd gone home
I'd have a smoke
before turning off the lights
those few hours before morning
my favourite time of night

AUNT ALICE

my aunt Alice died a couple months ago
Alice was one sister younger
than my mother Effie
in their huge family

Alice died of cancer
same as my mom
but before she died
my aunt Alice
drove men crazy

not sure how many times she married
but I know she drove
her first husband both mute and thirsty
her second drove into a stone wall without braking
instead of driving home
to her

but I shouldn't talk about things I do not know

I asked my dad one time
what it was about Alice
that drove men to madness
he said he didn't have a clue

I always thought she looked like
Billie Holiday
a beautiful flower
broken somewhere
deep inside

ANOTHER FUNERAL

another funeral this week
this one in Oshawa

the funeral home was downtown
beside a pool hall
and across the street
from a pizza joint

my aunt Dora was 82
I guess she'd had enough

I shook hands with her last husband
all elderly and bewildered
maybe husband number four
I'm not certain

I remember the sad ending
of husband number two
his drunken nose in a mud puddle
behind the old Woolworths
after he'd stolen
several bottles of Aqua Velva

doesn't much matter once it's done
a mud-puddle nap
or a hospital bed

ELEPHANTS IN SMITH FALLS

yesterday an old friend
invited me out for breakfast
he was leaving town
to move to Perth
and the arms of a woman
and that is a fine
and reasonable reason
to move anywhere

after our meal
he gave me a couple of books of poetry
one by a young woman
whose name escapes me
and the other
a ragged copy of Raymond Souster's
Elephants on Yonge Street
the jacket was in tatters
but it was a first edition
and one of the few Souster books
I didn't already have

it was a fine parting gift
Souster's elephants
reminding me of another small town
when K and I were on our bikes
and leaving town early

only to discover, at 6 a.m.
that the circus had arrived
and elephants were roaming
the back streets of Smith Falls

a quiet street
us cycling
and the elephants with their handlers
an unusual start to that particular day
but a good start
an omen
for all those miles we had to ride
before the next small town

STEEL-TOED BOOTS

the summer I worked as a labourer
for a construction company
that built bridges
I started with a brand-new pair
of steel-toed, steel-soled, boots

by the end of my second week
I was brown as my boots
my hands had quit bleeding
and I was looking forward
to my first big paycheque

I took my girlfriend
to the fanciest restaurant in town
and smiled when the bill came

by the end of the second month
I'd worn a hole in the bottoms
of my once-new boots
from walking on the steel rebar
we were tying into mats
before pouring the concrete

it was a matter of some pride
that I'd worked my boots to tatters
I gave my boss my full attention
all day long and did what I was told
when I was told to do it

I even jumped off that bridge one day
simply because my boss told me to
went into the water feet first
boots on

ODIN

Kirk Douglas sure looked fine
when he played a Viking as a young man

of course I was a sucker for Spartacus
all Daltony Trumbo wise and brave

when a Viking died in Kirk's movie
they put him on a ship
pushed the ship to open water
then sent a rainbow
of flaming arrows
to set it on fire
to light the way to Valhalla
and his visit
with Odin

it's different for me
for the past few years
the dog living next door
has made our home his second

when I open the front door
I hear him bound up our porch stairs
with the thundering footsteps of a god
his name is also Odin

my Odin has the same burnt orange
blond black flaming hair
as Kirk Douglas
all furry valiant in his Viking attire

Gods are never the deities
we think they are
and dogs rarely the people
we imagine them to be

THE RIVER ROAD TO LAKEFIELD

is where I thought
I would get my hands
on Carol Thomson's bra

there were six of us
crammed into Alan Seabrooke's mother's car
and we had parked, in the dark
near one of the locks on the river

Alan and his front-seat date
were resplendent with space
while the four of us
in the hatchback's small rear seat
wrestled as though
we were fighting in the gym

I might have fondled Carol's breast
but it could just as easily
have been someone else's elbow

thankfully
mosquitoes ended our brief masquerade
and our proximity to the river
and the eddies and the small pools
of water that produced flying squadrons
of unromantic bloodsuckers

we all mustered buttons and pride and vanity
in the shuffle of opened doors, lights
and then the slow parade home
to each of our quiet houses
where our parents
were smoking Belvederes
in the living room
and watching Johnny Carson
get drunk

PEPÉ LE PEW

we were sitting in front
of our campfire
at a provincial park
somewhere in Quebec
when a small skunk
came out of the dark
and walked through
the small space
between us
we were both
on the same side of the fire
sitting close enough
to hold hands

I tried to be still
and silent
with a big
"I told you so!"
in my eyes
and aimed at my wife

she was also trying
to be still
and silent
but mostly
trying not to laugh

I had been a reluctant camper
before Pepé Le Pew appeared
but at that point
I grabbed my sleeping bag
and a bottle
then moved into the cab
of our truck

I poured myself a drink
and set it on the dash
found a good station
on the radio
smiled
because I'd never have to
camp again

PING-PONG PLAYER

I only ever saw one stripper
who could shoot ping-pong balls
across the room with her twat

and I know that's not
a particularly delicate word
but no one ever shot
a ping-pong ball
across the room
and into Larry Preston's
Labatt's Blue
from a vagina

she was a tiny woman
with breasts that didn't need a bra
muscular thighs
and hair like a blond Brillo pad

no one in the room
paid much attention
when she put her quarters
into the jukebox
and spread her blanket
on the floor

but when she popped
that first ball
across the room
Paulie the Scarf

yelled "Hey look
she's laying eggs!"

that got everyone's attention
and little miss ping-pong
brought it home from there

her standing ovation
the one and only
I ever witnessed
in a peeler bar

DON CHERRY TALKS RELIGION

Don Cherry is ranting about a defenceman and the Lord
and it makes me want to puke Swiss Chalet and their
greasy chicken commercial across the screen   it's the
seventh game of the Stanley Cup finals and I am praying
to the hockey gods for my team and my team only   I've
been a hockey fan as long as I can remember and learned
to skate soon as I could walk   my father played hockey
for the Warsaw Flyers then for the army when he was
stationed in Europe I don't remember seeing him play
but he was usually the captain and that used to mean
something   my team is wearing red and white the
home team outfitted in black there's no score in the game
and it is well into the second period   somewhere else
men lined up to get into a shelter   huddled around
their cigarettes   one of them is wearing a team jacket
same colours as the team that just scored the opener

SPRING

talked to Bob's junkie daughter, Sara, this morning
she was dressed like a budget Helena Bonham Carter
and a little jumpy

an ambulance took her father away yesterday:
stage four brain cancer

Bob has been our neighbour for years
but until he retired last year
we never saw him much
and it doesn't look like
we'll see much more of him

Sara is in a methadone program
or was the last time Bob spoke to me about it
she seems lost on the sunniest days
as she rollerblades to the clinic
rolls back home

Bob was fine a couple of months ago
out shovelling the snow with the rest of us
telling our old-man lies
blowing our noses into hankies
and talking hopefully about spring

well, spring is here
and it hasn't helped Bob one bit

WE WERE EARLY IN OUR MARRIAGE

miles and miles from anywhere
on a hilly gravel road
our bikes
weighed down with camping gear
and I got to see
what my wife
was really made of

I was riding lead
and nearing the top
of a large hill
when a giant
black German shepherd
came out of the trees
that lined the road
on both sides
and lunged
teeth first
at my bike

animals see bikes
and their riders
as one large beast
the dog had latched
on to my sleeping bag
it was tied tightly
over my back wheel

the dog pulled me
and my bicycle
down to the road

my wife had been
some distance behind
but here she was
an angry version
and riding her kamikaze mountain bike
right into the furry belly
of the beast

the dog's owner appeared
seconds later
with a large shovel
that he used to further persuade
the dog to heel
eventually the monster
released his death grip

in that moment
I saw the fearlessness of love
and the ferocity
   had long suspected
 n my true love's conviction

 'd never felt safer
 r more loved·

"but I will not brake today for grace,
I round the reckless curve"
—Lynn Powell

"You ever do that,
take what you want just to see how it feels?"
—Susana H. Case

"And what if I did run
*   my ship aground;*
oh, still it was splendid
*   to sail it!"*
—Henrik Ibsen

ACKNOWLEDGEMENTS

Thanks to Brian and Karen and everyone at Anvil Press. Thanks to Kirsty for her perseverance. Thanks to Stuart and Laurie—Laurie for her perseverance and Stuart for everything else.

ABOUT THE AUTHOR

Born in London, Ontario, in 1956, Michael Dennis published his first poems in the early '70s. His work has appeared in scores of journals and more than 30 books and chapbooks. From 2013 to 2020, Michael wrote in-depth responses to 812 poetry books he admired on his blog, *Today's book of poetry.* His working life has included everything from stints in car plants and copper mines to installing artworks in galleries and doing time as a short-order cook and dishwasher in a strip club; he ran a small boutique hotel in the '80s, was Santa at the Kmart in Charlottetown one year, and opened a non-profit ESL school in Jablonec nad Nisou, Czechoslovakia, immediately following the Velvet Revolution. Michael has driven a taxi and a truck and had a brief stint as a private chauffeur. Now semi-retired, he lives in Ottawa.